I0155624

SONGS FOR THE
IRISH ROAD

A TRAVELING COMPANION TO A JOURNEY
ACROSS IRELAND WITH IRISH BALLADEER
PHILIP M. PRICE, DIGNIFIED HISTORIAN
DARRELL LEWIS, AND THE MADCAP
ALASKAN SENSATION, THE

Rogues & Wenches

BY N.J. HARRISON, LUCIA WOOFTER,
DARRELL LEWIS, PHILIP M. PRICE,
AND ROBERT WOOFTER

© 2015 by Access Education

ALL RIGHTS RESERVED.
No part of this work covered by the copyright hereon may be reproduced
or used in any form or by any means – graphic, electronic, or mechanical,
including photocopying, recording, taping, Web distribution or
information storage and retrieval systems – without the written
permission of the publisher.

All reasonable efforts have been made to contact the copyright holders for
the lyrics included within these pages. Anyone who believes their
copyright to be infringed is welcome to contact the publisher.

Songs for the Irish Road band photo provided by Tony D. Batres Band tour
logo designed by Kevin Hall. Band caricatures drawn by Greg Solomon.
Cover design by Natalie J. Harrison.

Photo credits: Tony D. Batres, pages 1, 7, 9, 22, 37, 62, 71, 77, 87, 91, and
92; Darrell Lewis and Andrea Axelson, pages 4, 28, and 47; Natalie
Harrison, page 10, 14, 23, 27, 31, 58, 67, 79, 84, and 92; Guinness
Storehouse, page 13; Wikimedia Commons, page 17, 32, 39, ; Tolpuddle
Martyr's Museum, page 65; Michael Dineen, 91; Lucia Woofter, pages 40
and 68; Joyce Bennett, page 23; Charity Edwards, pages 23 and 58; Nikki
Harkins, page 23; Philip Price, page 43 and 73; David Price, pages 50, 55
and 61; and Brett Woofter, page 58.

ISBN 978-1-934231-06-7

5201 E Northern Lights Blvd, Suite 1W
Anchorage, AK 99508
www.accesseducationpress.com.

Access
EDUCATION

Acknowledgements

The publishers of *Songs for the Irish Road* thank Alaska-based and Irish-born balladeer Philip M. Price for coming up with the inspirational idea for this fun songbook project and contributing the lyrics and chords for the traditional and original songs he sings; Lucia Woofter of Rogues & Wenches fame for being the tireless originator and organizer of the Rogues & Wenches 2013 and 2015 Ireland Tours, for writing the book's introduction page and two song introductions, and for providing the lyrics and chords for the traditional songs the Rogues & Wenches sing; Robert Woofter for providing legal and song selection support for the songbook; Darrell Lewis for writing the many wonderful historical passages spread throughout the pages to follow; and Natalie Harrison for spearheading the songbook project, designing the book's exterior and interior, and writing the section introductions, tourism segments, photo captions, and song introductions.

The publishers also thank those who provided the book's many wonderful pictures, including Tony D. Batres, Andrea Axelson and Darrell Lewis, Lucia and Robert Woofter, David Price, Philip Price, Charity Edwards, Brett Woofter, Joyce Bennett, Nikki Harkins, and Natalie Harrison.

Access Education Press, 2015

TABLE OF CONTENTS

About this Book

What makes *Songs for the Irish Road* unique and not just
another collection of traditional Irish songs? It is a musical
travelogue of a journey across Ireland. Our concept was to
make our first tour of the Emerald Isle come alive with
songs and ballads about the very places we were visiting,
the characters who lived there, and the historical events that
left their mark on the Irish landscape and psyche. With that
in mind we selected our songs and organized the book
geographically according to the sites, monuments, villages
or bodies of water we saw during our tour.

When the authors sat down to coffee on a late summer
afternoon in 2012, we were faced with the daunting task of
picking just a few traditional, original, and contemporary
Irish songs out of the hundreds we know and love. We
chose songs that lend themselves to sing-a-longs, songs
whose choruses are lilting, memorable, and easy to sing.

This project has been a labor of love and we has
embellished it with photos of our 2013 so that when you
are at home or sitting around the campfire with a guitar,
you, too, can play that special tune and experience an
Ireland sojourn in "forty shades of green."

THE VOYAGE TO IRELAND

As we start our musical voyage across the Emerald Isle, we first whet our melodic appetite with a few songs about Ireland. The first is a traditional song calling us back to the Irish homeland ("Come to the Bower"), followed by songs about drinking ("The Wild Rover" and "Whiskey, You're the Devil"), politics ("The Orange and the Green"), and the predicament of being an Irish spinster ("Old Maid in the Garrett"). This section concludes with a drinking song about Ireland's national treasure, Guinness stout ("Back in the Clydesdale").

In each of the sections to follow, there is a map highlighting where we are in our musical journey and the locations named in the each of the songs.

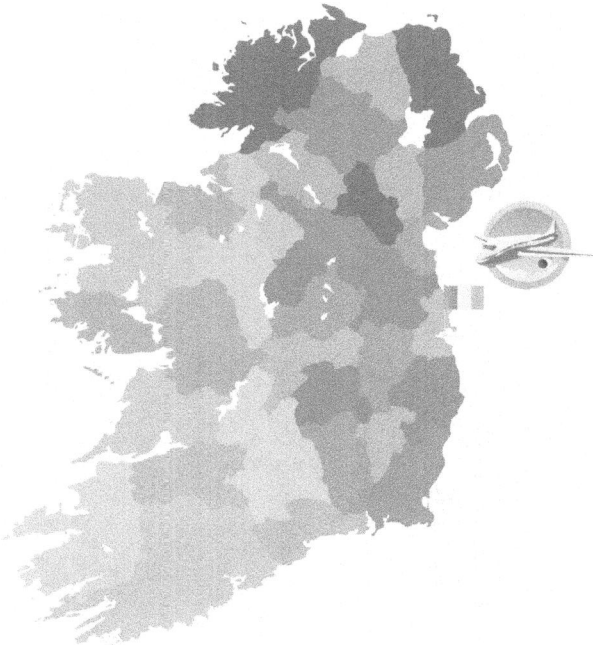

WILL YOU COME TO THE BOWER *(traditional)*

We start our musical journal across Ireland with this traditional song that was popular in 19th century inviting Irish-American listeners to return to help the Emerald Isle in its struggle for freedom. *Bower*, by definition an attractive dwelling or shelter, refers to the Irish homeland.

Full of poetic references to Ireland's history of struggle and stunning geography, "Will You Come to the Bower" is still a popular favorite in Ireland today.

```
D                       A                        D
Will you come to the bower, o'er the free boundless ocean
D                       A                        D
Where the stupendous waves roll in thundering in motion,
D                       Bm          D          A
Where the mermaids are seen, and the fierce tempest gathers,
D                       Bm
To love Erin the green, the dear land of our fathers.
```

[Chorus]
```
D                       A                        D
Will you come, will you, will you, will you come to the Bower.
```

Stupendous waves crashing against the Cliffs of Moher on the west coast of Ireland

[2]

Will you come to the land of O'Neill and O'Donnell,
Of Lord Lucan the bold, and the immortal O'Connell,
Where Brian drove the Danes, and St.Patrick the vermin,
And whose valleys remain, still most beautiful and charming.

[3]

You can visit Dublin city, and the fine groves of Blarney
The Ban, Boyne, the Liffey, and the lakes of Killarney.
You may ride on the tide, o're the broad majestic Shannon.
You may sail round Lough Neigh, and see storied
Dungannon.

[4]

You can visit New Ross, gallant Wexford and Gorey,
Where the green was last seen by proud Saxon and Tory,
Where the soil is sanctified, by the blood of each true man
Where they died satisfied,t heir enemies they would not run
from.

[5]

You can visit Benburb and the storied Blackwater,
Where Owen Roe met Monroe and his chieftains did
slaughter.
Where the lambs sport and play on the mossy all over,
From those golden bright views,to enchanting Rostrevor.

[6]

Will you come and awake our lost land from its slumber
And her fetters we will break, links that long have
encumbered,
And the air will resound, with Hosanna to greet you,
On the shore will be found gallant Irishmen to meet you.

THE WILD ROVER *(traditional)*

This song is a delightful traditional Irish folk song which dates back to the early sixteenth century and has been popular over the centuries with North Atlantic fishing crews. Because it is fun, easy to sing, and includes audience participation and clapping on the chorus, "The Wild Rover" can still be heard in Irish pubs around the world.

[Chorus]
And it's No, Nay, Never, No, Nay Never, No more.
Will I play the wild rover. No Never, No more.

     E   **A**
I've been a wild rover for many's the year.
     B   **B7**   **E**
I've spent all me money on whiskey and beer.
                               A
And now I'm returning with gold in great store.
     E   **B**   **B7**   **E**
And I never will play the wild rover no more.

I went to an ale house I used to frequent.
I told the landlady my money was spent.
I asked for credit; she answered me "Nay!
Such custom as yours I can have any day."

I reached in my pocket for ten sovereigns bright,
The landlady's eyes opened wide with delight.
She said, "I have whiskey and wines of the best."
Then she took me upstairs and showed me the rest.

I'll go to my parents; confess what I've done,
I'll ask them to pardon their prodigal son.
If they take me back as ofttimes before,
Then I just might go play the wild rover once more.

WHISKEY, YOU'RE THE DEVIL *(traditional)*

The word *whiskey* actually comes from the Gaelic word *uisce beatha* and means "the water of life."

[Chorus]

D   G
Whiskey, you're the devil, you're leading me astray,
        D   E7   A7
Over hills and mountains and to Americay,
      D   G
You're sweeter, stronger, decenter, you're spunkier than tay,
    D   G   D   Bm Em A7 D
O, whiskey, you're my darling, drunk or sober.

[BRIDGE]

 D
O, love, fare thee well, with me ti-ther-ee-i, doo-dle-um-a-dah
    Em
With me ti-ther-ee-i, doo-dle-um-a-dah
  Bm   G   D   G   D   A7   D
Me right-fol toor-a-laddie, o, there's whiskey in the jar.

  D
O, now brave boys we'll run for march
   Em   A7
And not to Portugal or Spain,
   Bm   D
The drums are beating, banners flying,
   E7   A7
The devil at home we'll find tonight.

Oh, the French are fighting boldly,
Men are dying hot and cowardly,
Give every man his flask of power,
His firelock on his shoulder.

Says the mother, "Do not wrong me,
Don't take my daughter from me,
For if you do I shall torment you,
And after that me ghost will haunt you!"

THE ORANGE AND THE GREEN *(Anthony Murphy)*

What happens when a Catholic lass weds a Protestant lad in
Ireland? This musical answer emphasizes the humor of this
rather confusing situation.

[Chorus]
Oh, it is the biggest mix-up that you have ever seen,
My father, he was Orange and me mother, she was Green.

       D   **A**
Oh, my father was an Ulsterman, proud Protestant was he.
  G   **D**   **A**   **D**
My mother was a Catholic girl from County Cork, was she.
                          A
They were married in two churches; lived happily enough
  G   **D**   **A**   **D**
Until the day when I was born, when things got rather tough.

[2]
Baptized by Father Ivey, I was rushed away by car,
To be made a little Orangeman, my father's shining star.
I was christened "David Anthony" but still in spite of that
To my father I was "William," while me mother called me
"Pat".

[3]
With my mother every Sunday, to Mass I'd proudly stroll,
Then later on the Orange lads would try to save my soul.
Though both sides tried to claim me, well, I was smart
because
I'd play the flute or play the harp, depending where I was.

[4]

Now when I'd sing those rebel songs much to me mother's joy,

Me father would jump up and say, "Look here, would you, me boy!

That's quite enough of that lad." He'd then toss me a coin

He'd have me sing The Orange Flute or the Heros of the Boyne.

[5]

One day my ma's relations came 'round to visit me,

Just as my father's kinfolk were sitting down to tea.

We tried to smooth things over but they began to fight

And me being strictly neutral, I bashed everyone in sight!

[6]

My parents never could agree about my type of school,

My learning was all done at home, that's why I'm such a fool.

They both passed on, God rest them, but left me caught between,

That awful color problem of the Orange and the Green.

Old Maid in the Garrett (Martin Packer, traditional)

Unlike today, there was once a significant social stigma attached to reaching a certain age unmarried. A *garret* is the attic room of a house, where many older unmarried Irish women lived in the homes of their married relatives. This classic Irish favorite tells the tale of a plucky Irish spinster who decides to get a parrot if she can't get a man.

The lyrics for "Old Maid in the Garrett" were written by Martin Packer in the nineteenth century and the tune was written at least 200 years earlier in the seventeenth century. Although the correct spelling is with one *t*, the song's titular "garrett" has traditionally been spelled with two.

LISDOONVARNA
HOME OF THE FAMOUS
MATCHMAKING
FESTIVAL

The town of Lisdoonvarna in County Clare, Ireland is famous for its annual Matchmaking Festival. Held over multiple weekends in September, approximately 40,000 singles come to Lisdoonvarna with a hopeful gleam in their eyes.

Lisdoonvarna began as a spa town in the mid-eighteenth century because it was located on mineral springs. As more and more people came to the town for a rest, it became a hotspot for matchmaking the area's unmarried farmers who saw few women on their solitary country farms. By the 1920s, matchmaking had become a well established tradition in the area.

D
I have often heard it said from me father and me mother
     A   **G**   **D**
That going to a wedding is the making of another.
D   **G**   **D**
Well, if this be so, then I'll go without a biddin'
                                       A
O kind providence, won't you send me to a wedding.

[Chorus]
          D   **G**   **D**   **G**
And its Oh dear me, how would it be,
 D   **A**   **D**
If I die an old maid in a garrett.

[2]

Well, there's my sister Jean, she's not handsome or good
looking,

Scarcely sixteen and a fella she was courting.

Now at twenty-four with a son and a daughter,

Here am I at forty-five and I've never had an offer.

[3]

I can cook and I can sew and I can keep the house right tidy,

Rise up in the morning and get the breakfast ready.

There's nothing in this whole world would make me half so
cheery

As a wee fat man to call me his own deary.

[4]

Well now I'm away home for nobody's heeding,

Nobody's heeding and nobody's pleading.

I'll go away to my own bitty garret

If I can't get a man, then I'll have to get a parrot.

BACK IN THE CLYDESDALE *(Mike Campbell)*

This song was written by one of Alaska's own, Mike
Campbell, who is now living in retirement in Florida. Mike, a
singer and songwriter, first debuted this tune at one of
Seamus Kennedy's concerts at St. Patrick's parish in
Anchorage, Alaska, and to preface his song he called out to
the Rogues & Wenches, who were in the audience and said
"this one's for you" and he was right!

[Chorus]
Oh, put that Budweiser back in the Clydesdale,
It's not the right flavor for me.
The color's all wrong and there's not enough foam
And it's got all the kick of weak tea.
Now pull me a pint of that good Guinness stout
With a body you cannot see through.
Put that Budweiser back in the Clydesdale, boys,
And pour me a beer that is true!

    C
I went to the pub after working all day,
    F   **C**
And I ordered a slow Guinness stout
    F   **C**   **Am**
But the yuppies were yapping so loud on their cell phones
    D7   **G7**
The barman did not hear me shout.
    C
He brought me a glass and a bottle of Bud,
    F   **G7**
And set them down in front of me,
    F   **C**   **A7**
Well, I coughed and I sputtered in pure disbelief
    D7   **G7**   **C**
And I sang out this chorus with glee.

[2]

Then the waitress came by when I'd finished my first one,
A frazzled young woman named Jill,
She snatched up my empty without even looking,
And went off to get a refill.
She brought back a glass of some pale liquid garbage
And said, "Here's the Bud you asked for."
Well, I gave her a glare that would knock down a horse
Then I sang out this chorus once more.

[3]

So if ever you're seeking a beer with good flavor,
To round out your day or your meal,
And they serve you a Millers, a Coors or a Bud
Or some other brand that ain't real.
If the "King of Beers" is your only selection
I hope that you'll answer like this,
Put that Budweiser back in the the Clydesdale, boys,
I don't drink twelve ounces of ... (that lousy beer)!

All around the world, Ireland has become synonymous with dark, rich Guinness beer. When visiting Dublin, you can visit the Guinness Storehouse, an old brewing facility that has been converted into a seven-story, world-class museum. At the Storehouse, you can see how Dublin's most delectable nectar is made and you can even sample a pint of the black stuff!

The Celts

The Celts are part of an Indo-European group of nomadic people that began migrating from the dry grasslands north of the Caucasus Mountains about 4,000 BP. They migrated in waves that included Germans, Slavs, Greeks, and Celts, among others. The distinctive Celtic culture first appeared in current day Switzerland and southwest Germany about 3,200 BP, and expanded throughout Europe by about 2,300 BP. As it expanded, it further subdivided into groups with differing Celtic dialects. With the rise of the Roman Empire in about 2,100 BP, and then the Slav and Germanic peoples, the Celts were pushed to the northwestern fringe of Europe. It was at this time that the Celts established themselves in Ireland and began their 2,000 year march toward what we know today as the Irish.

GALWAY

Our first stop on our musical journey through Ireland is at Galway, located in County Galway in the western province of Connacht. It's the fourth biggest city in Ireland and home to a lively traditional music scene.

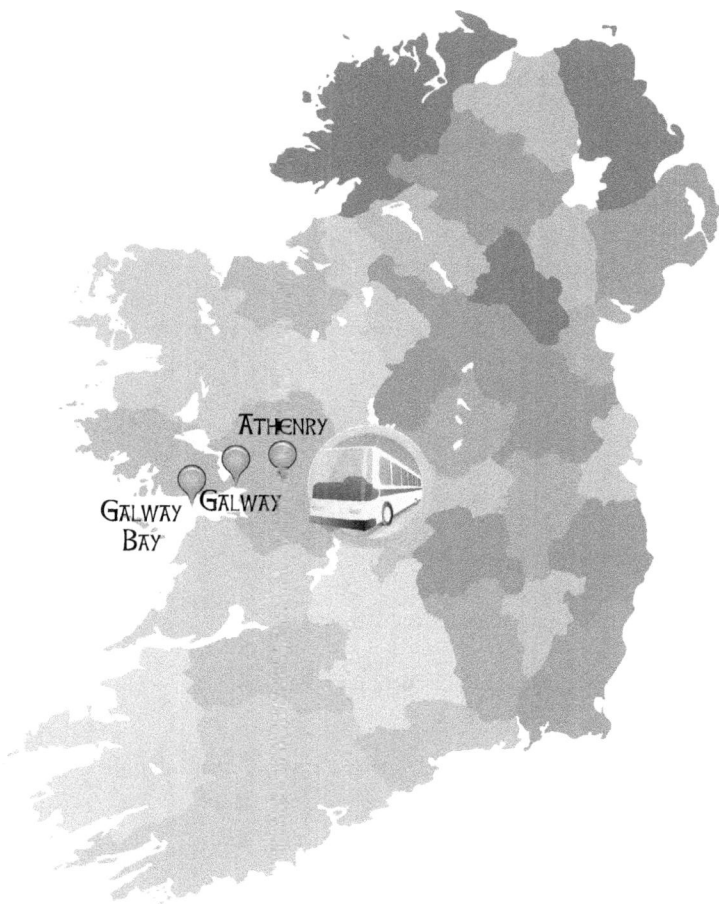

ATHENRY

GALWAY

GALWAY
BAY

FIELDS OF ATHENRY *(Peter St. John)*

The Rogues & Wenches' version of this song was arranged by Erin Wells and moves gradually through two modulations, giving an uplifting feel of hope to an otherwise heartbreaking farewell. The arrangement is emotionally potent as Erin and Ben sing the lover's parting dialog in duet to one another, murmuring a farewell that will echo a lifetime.

[Chorus]

C   F C   Am
Low lie the fields of Athenry,
 C   G
Where once we watched the small free birds fly.
 C   F
Our love was on the wing,
 C   G
We had dreams and songs to sing
                                 C
It's so lonely 'round the Fields of Athenry.

C   F   C   G
By a lonely prison wall I heard a young girl calling.
C   F   G
"Michael, they are taking you away,
C   F
For you stole Trevelyn's corn,
 C   G
So the young might see the morn.
                             C
Now a prison ship lies waiting in the bay."

[2]

By a lonely prison wall, I heard a young man calling,
"Nothing matters, Mary, when you're free!
Against the Famine and the Crown
I rebelled, they ran me down.
Now you must raise our child with dignity.

[3]

By a lonely harbor wall, she watched the last star falling,

As that prison ship sailed out against the sky.

Sure she'll wait and hope and pray

For her love in Botany Bay.

It's so lonely 'round the Fields of Athenry.

Although written in the 1970s, "The Fields of Athenry" is set during the Great Irish Famine in the mid-nineteenth century. It tells the story of a man who was sentenced and being sent to the penal colony in Australia for stealing food to feed his starving family. The "Trevelyan" mentioned in the song is Charles Edward Trevelyan, a senior British colonial administrator in charge of "famine relief," who said that the famine was a "mechanism for reducing surplus population" in Ireland. He remains one of the most detested British figures in Irish history.

The Famine Memorial at the Custom House Keys in Dublin

The Famine

When the Great Famine struck in 1845, conditions in Ireland were ripe for such a tragedy. Absentee English landlords had forced Irish tenant farmers to subsist on ever shrinking plots of land for ever increasing rents. Because potatoes thrived in Ireland, farmers could dedicate most of their land to growing cash crops, primarily grain, to pay their rents. By the 1840s, nearly half of Ireland's population was living on the margins, solely dependent on the potato for food. The airborne fungus blew in from England in fall 1845 and rapidly spread to half the potato crop, causing the leaves to blacken and potatoes to rot in the ground. Crops failed entirely in 1846, 1848, and 1849, and an estimated 1.5 million people died of starvation and associated diseases during this period. Counties such as Galway, Mayo, and Clare were hardest hit, with an estimated 50,000-60,000 people per year perishing. Nearly a million escaped the misery by emigrating to Canada, the United States, England, Scotland, and Wales, while others, unable to pay for passage, committed crimes in order to get sent to penal colonies in Australia and New Zealand. Ireland's population was reduced from 8.2 million in 1841 to 6.5 million in 1850.

GALWAY SHAWL *(traditional)*

Rogues & Wenches recorded "Galway Shawl" on their first album *Spirits*. Verse three refers to an "Irish Linnet," a small finch known for its melodious song. Because of this reference we now use the moniker "Irish Linnet" to refer to Rogues & Wenches' own song bird, wench Erin Kathleen.

[Chorus]
She wore no jewels, nor costly diamonds,
No paint nor powder, no, none at all.
She wore a bonnet with ribbon on it,
And round her shoulder was a Galway shawl.

G   **Em**
In Oranmore, in the County Galway,
          C   **Am**   **D**
One pleasant evening in the month of May,
         G   **Em**
I spied a damsel, she was young and handsome
        C   **D**   **G**
Her beauty fairly took my breath away.

[2]
We went on walking, she went on talking,
'Till her father's cottage came into view.
Says she: "Come in, sir, and meet my father,
And for to please him play The Foggy Dew."

[3]
I played The Blackbird and Stacks of Barley,
And Rodney's Courage and The Foggy Dew.
She sang each note like an Irish linnet,
And tears flowed from her eyes so blue.

[4]
"Twas early, early, all in the morning,
I hit the road for old Donnegal.
Said she, "Goodbye, sir." She cried and kissed me,
And my heart remains with that Galway shawl.

LET THE GRASSES GROW *(E. Harrigan and D. Braham)*

"Let the Grasses Grow," also known as "The Rare Old Mountain Dew," was written for a Dublin play, *The Blackbird*, that was published in 1882. The song praises poitín, the alcohol produced illegally by Irish moonshiners. The distillation of poitín, typically 60% to 90% alcohol by volume, was outlawed in 1661. In 1997, the Irish Revenue Commissioners decided to allow this potent brew to be sold under license in Ireland.

[Chorus]
Let the grasses grow and the waters flow in a free and easy way,
But give me enough of the rare old stuff that's made near Galway Bay.
And policemen all from Donegal, Sligo and Leitrim, too.
We'll give them the slip and we'll take a sip of the rare old mountain dew.

G   **C**   **G**
At the foot of the hill there's a neat little still where the smoke curls
       D
up to the sky.

G   **C**   **G**   **D**   **G**
By a whiff of a smell you can plainly tell there's a poitín still nearby.

                                    C
Oh it fills the air with a perfume rare and betwit both me and you

G   **C**   **G**   **D**   **G**
As home we roll we can drink a bowl or a bucket of mountain dew.

Now learned men who use the pen have wrote the praises high,
Of the sweet poitín from Ireland green, distilled from wheat and rye.
Away with pills, it'll cure all ills of Pagan, Christian or Jew.
So take off your coat and grease your throat with the real old mountain dew.

THE WEST

From Galway, we explore the rest of the west of Ireland. Unlike Dublin and the east of Ireland, the west is mostly rural, with only 30% of the population living in urban areas. Must of the beautiful countryside in the west is also part of a Gaeltacht, which is an officially recognized region that actively attempts to restore the traditional Irish language and culture. Listen closely and you might pick up a few words of Irish!

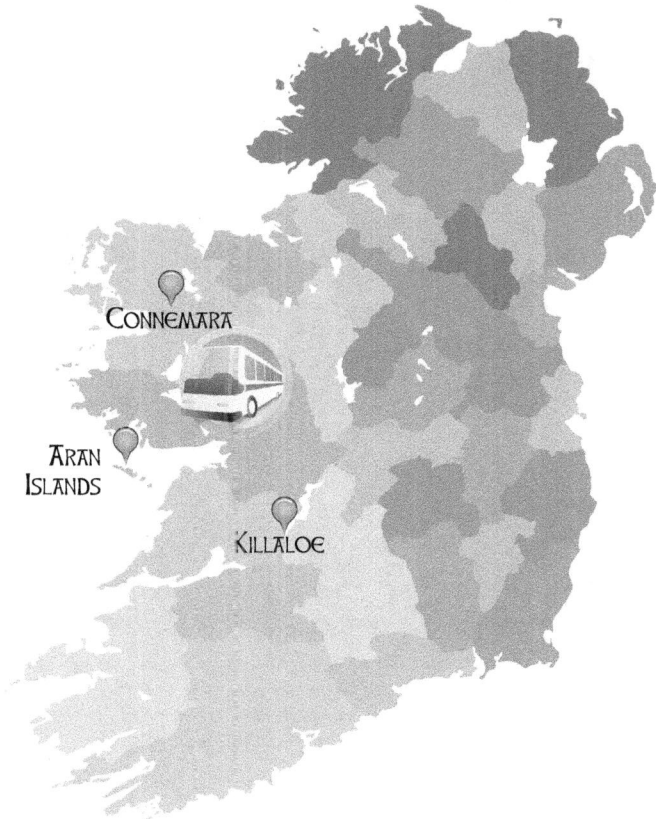

CONNEMARA

ARAN ISLANDS

KILLALOE

When you're in the hills of the west of Ireland, keep an eye out for leprechauns!

Erin and Ben of the Rogues & Wenches engaged in a battle over poitín.
Poitín was a potent Irish moonshine also called "mountain tay," or
mountain tea, perhaps because poitín stills were hidden from "Excise
men," or tax collectors, in the Irish mountainsides.

Every trip to the West should include stopping in for a pint at Sean's Bar, Ireland's oldest pub dating back to 900 AD, and taking a boat trip across the waters to the Aran Islands.

THE BEGGARMAN *(traditional)*

Many of the early beggarmen in Ireland descended from the journeymen tradesmen and traveling musicians who traveled the countryside looking for a bit of work, a plate of warm grub, and a soft bed for a night or two. For centuries, people of the Irish countryside have been known for providing a warm welcome to traveling strangers. This song about a jolly, little beggarman has been a signature song at Philip Price's performances for the past fifty years.

D   **C**
I'm a little beggarman, a begging I have been,
        D   **C**
And for three score or more, in this little isle of green.
D   **D**
Known from the Liffey, down to Killaloe,
       D
I'm known by the name now of old Johnny Dhu.
   C
Of all the trades a going, sure begging is the best,
      D   **C**
Ah, when a man is tired, he can sit him down and rest.
      D   **C**
He begs for his supper, he's got nothing else to do,
      D
But roll around the corner with his old rig-a-doo.

[Chorus]
 C
Nya nya nootin nitin nya,
       D   **C**
Diddly ootil itil ootil itil dootil itin nya,
D   **C**
Nootil nitin dootin ditil diddly itin dah,
      D
Diddly ootin ditin dootin nitin nootin nyi nya.

[2]

Slept in a barn way down in Mullabawn,

The night being dark, and the rain coming on.

The holes in the roof, and the rain coming through,

The cats and the rats they were playing peek a boo.

Now who should awaken, but the woman of the house,

With her white spotted apron, and her calico blouse.

She began to frighten when I said boo!

Don't be afraid Ma'am, it's only Johnny Dhu.

[3]

I met a little flaxen haired girl one day.

"Good morning, little flaxen haired girl," I did say.

"Good morning, little beggarman, and how do you do,

"With your rags and your tags and your auld rigadoo?"

"I'll buy a pair of leggings and a collar and a tie,

"And a nice young lady I'll meet by and by.

"I'll buy a pair of goggles and I'll color them with blue.

"An old fashioned lady, I will make out of you."

[4]

Its over the roads with me baggage on me back,

And it's down through the fields with me old grey sack.

Holes in me shoes and me toes peeping through,

And all round the corner with me auld rigadoo.

I must be going to bed for it's getting late at night.

The fire's all out and out goes the light.

Now you've heard the story of my auld rigadoo,

So good night and God be with you now from auld Johnny Dhu.

THE MONK *(Philip M. Price)*

Philip Price wrote this song way back in the 1970's for a
Dublin friend who went off to join the seminary to become a
pious man of the cloth. This soon-to-be holy man was
known for heavy smoking, gargling (Dublin slang for
drinking), and chasing women. He didn't last long at the
seminary before he was up to his old tricks again!

```
       G                        D
Left me home one Friday to be a pious monk.
                              C                   G
Left behind me weaknesses of girls and getting drunk.
                        D
Went with a good will to live me life in prayer,
                            C              G
But that same night I went courting in the air.
```

[Chorus]
```
         C                        G
And its courting in the night air's no life for a monk,
    D                     C           G
Courting in the night air and getting drunk.
    G                     D
Creeping in at two a.m., collapsing on me bunk,
                          C           G
Never had a better time till I became a monk..
```

[2]

And its courting in the night air's no life for a monk.
Courting in the night air and getting drunk.
Creeping in at two am, collapsing on me bunk,
Never had a better time, till I became a monk.

[3]

One day the baldy head monk, he called out me name,
Begging me to repent and the devil's name to shame.

Philip (right) performing "The Monk" with John Walsh and Ben Saylor at a session at Celtic Treasures in Anchorage, Alaska.

He preached such a sermon, that me heart it felt sore,
But that same night I went courting like before.

[4]
Went by the back streets unto the local town,
And into a pub and I starts to seat me down,
And there I saw a sight and I knew I wasn't drunk,
With a girl on each knee, was me baldy head monk.

[5]
Now every week night, at about half eight,
I climb the Abbey's towering walls and outside I wait,
Till along comes a baldy monk, deep in his prayer,
And we both go a courting in the clear night air.

Dun Aonghasa

Dun Aonghasa, on Inishmore, is the largest of several Bronze Age prehistoric stone forts located on the Aran Islands. Dating back 3,500 years and inhabited until about 900 AD, little is known about the inhabitants. The size of the fort (enclosing over 14 acres) and discovery of glass, stone, ivory, bone, and amber beads suggests a great deal of wealth. Amber and glass came from the Baltic and Middle East, respectively, and would have been acquired through trade. Bronze rings, swords, knives, spearheads, axe heads and clay molds for their manufacture have been discovered at Dun Aonghasa and further exemplifies the wealth of Dun Aonghasa's inhabitants. Evidence of these Bronze Age peoples has been found throughout Ireland and the bronze tools and jewelry they fashioned has been found as far away as Scandinavia and the European continent.

KERRY

County Kerry is known for its striking scenery and for the fact that it's Dingle Peninsula contains the westernmost point in Ireland. In addition to a lively music and football (soccer) scene, Kerry is full of many historical points of interest. Our personal favorite is the Muckross House, a Victorian era mansion that lets you explore mansion life both upstairs and downstairs.

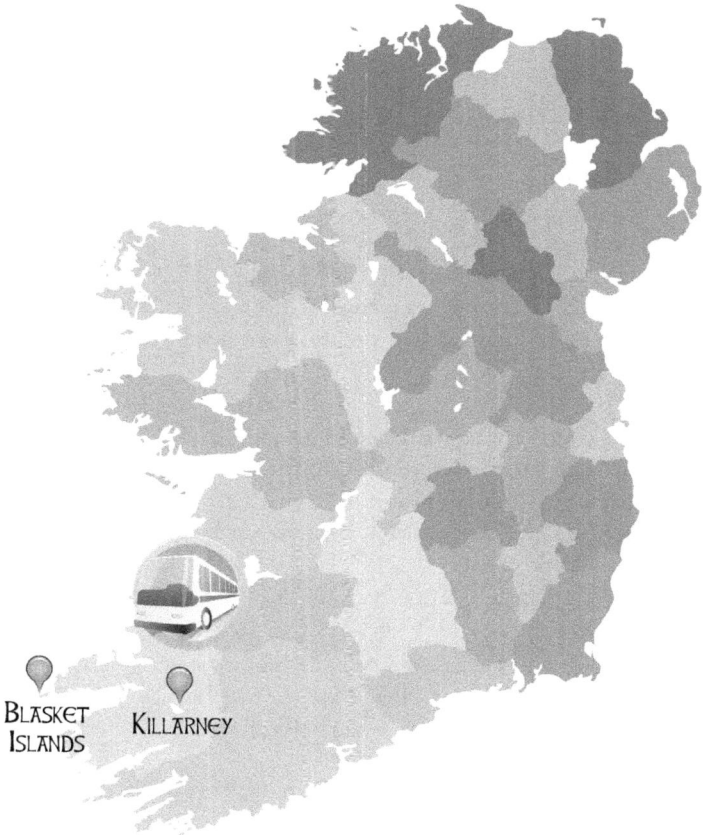

BLASKET
ISLANDS

KILLARNEY

MUIRSHIN DURKIN *(traditional)*

This popular Irish folk song tells the story of a many who leaves Ireland and heads for California during the God Rush of 1849. *Muirshin* is the Gaelic equivalent of the name "Martin."

```
D                       A                         D
In the days I went a courtin' I was never tired resortin'
   D                A                              D
To an ale-house or a playhouse and many's the house besides.
   D                A                              D
But I told me brother Seamus I'd go off and be right famous
   D            A                          D
And I never would return again 'til I roamed the world wide.
```

[Chorus]
Goodbye Muirsheen Durkin, sure I'm sick and tired of working.
No more I'll dig the praties and no longer I'll be fooled.
As sure's me name is Carney I'll be off to California
Where instead of diggin' praties, I'll be diggin' lumps of gold.

[2]
I've courted girls in Blarney, in Kanturk, and in Killarney,
In Passage and in Queenstown, that is the Cobh of Cork.
Goodbye to all this pleasure, I'll be off to take me leisure
And the next time that you hear from me will be a letter from New York.

[3]
Goodbye to the girls at home, I'm going far across the foam
To try and make me fortune in far Amerikay.
There's gold and jewels a-plenty for the poor and for the gentry,
And when I return again I never more will say...

Red Is the Rose *(traditional)*

This traditional Irish song is sung to the same tune as the
Scottish ballad "Loch Lomond."

[Chorus]
Red is the rose that in yonder garden grows,
And fair is the lily of the valley.
Clear is the water that flows from the Boyne,
But my love is fairer than any.

  D   **Em**   **G**
Come over the hills, my bonnie Irish lass,
         D   **G A**
Come over the hills to your darling.
 G   **D**   **G**   **Em**
You choose the rose, love, and I'll make the vow,
     D   **G**   **A7 D**
And I'll be your true love forever.

[2]
'Twas down by Killarney's green woods that
we strayed.
And the moon and the stars they were
shining.
The moon shone its rays on her locks of
golden hair,
And she swore she'd be my love forever.

[3]
It's not for the parting that my sister pains,
It's not for the grief of my mother,
'Tis all for the loss of my bonnie Irish lass,
That my heart is breaking forever.

Muckross House

Muckross House was constructed in 1843 by Henry Arthur Herbert. The Herberts moved to Ireland from Wales in the 1600s and amassed a fortune mining copper in the Muckross Peninsula and on Ross Island. In the 1770s, they inherited large estates from the MacCarthy family. Muckross House represents the pinnacle of their wealth.

Henry Herbert extensively renovated the 65 room Tudor Style mansion in the 1850s in preparation for Queen Victoria's visit in 1861. The Herberts declined into financial ruin in the late 1800s and in 1898, the mansion and the more than 47,000 acres on which it sat were purchased by Lord Ardilaun, a member of the Guinness family. After a short period, it was purchased as a wedding gift by California businessman William Bourn for his daughter Maud. After her death in 1932, her husband, Arthur Vincent, bequeathed the estate to County Kerry, saying, "Muckross estate would make a public park such as any country might be proud of."

THE BLASKET'S SOUND *(Philip M. Price)*

"The Blasket's Sound" is the story of a homeless man Philip Price met in London who was originally from Kerry. The man left Ireland as a young man to work in construction in England but lamented that he never made it back home.

Dm   **C**   **Dm**
As darkness descends over London, and the wind from the Thames start to blow,
Dm   **C**   **Dm**
I think of my young days in Ireland and homeward I'm longing to go,
F   **Am**   **C**   **Dm**
To stand on the banks of some river where peace and quiet are found,
Dm   **C**   **Dm**
Or sit out on a lone beach in Kerry, just listenin' to the Blasket's Sound.

[2]

As the rain drizzles down from the heavens and car lights flash through the dark,

I sit so cold and hungry alone all alone in the park,

If only when I was a young man, I'd not left to roam England round,

I'd be at home now in Ireland, just listening to the Blasket's Sound.

[3]

As reflections return to my sad eyes and years start to roll and fall,

I curse the day I departed to answer Mc Alpine's call,

I curse the women and liquor so free when you have the pound

And I rue that past day dearly, I left home and the Blasket's Sound.

[4]

As the park attendant he signals that the park is ready to close,

I make my way through London to where my God only knows,

And still inside is my yearning to return to my own native ground,

I'd swap noise and factory hooters, for waves and the Blasket's Sound.

The Blarney Stone

The Blarney Stone, or Stone of Destiny, is surrounded in legend and mystery. One legend says it that the Blarney Stone is one half of the Stone of Scone upon which the first King of Scots was seated in 847. It is said that it was presented to Cormac McCarthy by Robert the Bruce in 1314 as a gift for supporting the Scots in the Battle of Bannockburn. The Stone was set into the tower of Blarney Castle in 1446.

The earliest use of the word blarney is attributed to Queen Elizabeth I (1553-1603), in referring to Cormac Teige McCarthy's response to her request for an oath of loyalty. Cormac heaped praise and flattery upon the Queen, but came short of taking an oath. "Blarney, Blarney, I will hear no more of this Blarney!" was the Queen's response and today legend has it that kissing the Blarney Stone will give a person the gift of gab.

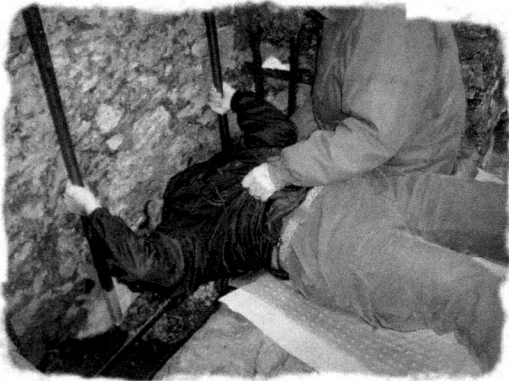

Just what every lawyer needs - the gift of gab! Bob of the Rogues & Wenches is pictured hanging upside down to kiss the Blarney Stone.

CORK

Our musical journey takes us next to County Cork, home of the famed Blarney stone at Blarney Castle, the historic Rock of Cashel, and Cobh, the port city from which more than six million people emigrated from Ireland.

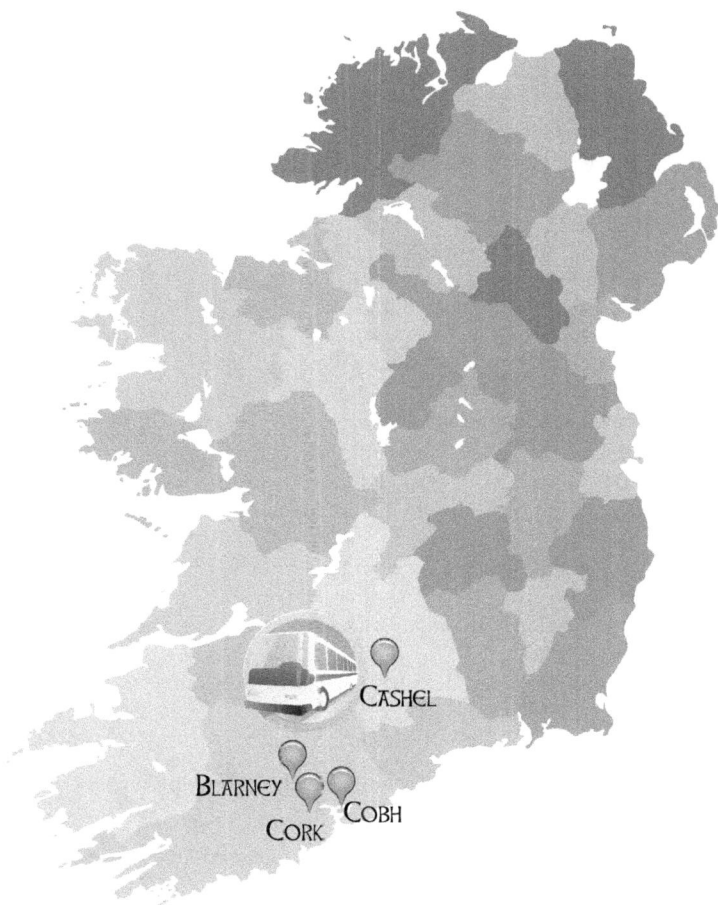

WHISKEY IN THE JAR *(traditional)*

One of the more famous Irish traditional songs worldwide, "Whiskey in the Jar" takes place in the southern mountains of Cork and Kerry. It recounts the story of a highwayman, who faces the ultimate betrayal at the hands his lover. This centuries-old song may have been based on the true story of an Irish highwayman who was executed in 1650.

Throughout the second half of the twentieth century, the tune has been recorded by many artists, including Thin Lizzy, the Dubliners, Burl Ives, Roger Whittaker, the Irish Rovers, Christy Moore, Celtic Thunder, and Metallica, who all sang cover versions of this song, each with slightly different lyrics. Here's the Rogues & Wenches' favorite version.

[Chorus]

A7
Mush-a ring dum-a do dum-a da
D   **G**
Wack fall the daddy-o, wack fall the daddy-o
          D   **A7**   **D**
There's whiskey in the jar.

   D   **Bm**
As I was a goin' over the far famed Kerry mountains
   G   **D**
I met with Captain Farrell and his money he was counting.
                                         Bm
I first produced me pistol and I then produced me rapier
          G   **D**
Saying "Stand and deliver!" for I am a bold deceiver.

[2]

I counted out his money and it made a pretty penny.
I put it in me pocket and I took it home to Jenny.
She sighed and she swore that she never would deceive me
But the devil take the women for they never can be easy.

[3]

I went up to me chamber, all for to take a slumber
And dreamt of gold and jewels and for sure 'twas no wonder.
But Jenny blew me chargers when she filled them up with water,
Then sent for Captain Farrell to be ready for the slaughter.

[4]

'Twas early in the morning, before I rose to travel.
Up comes a band of footmen and like wise Captain Farrell.
I first produced me pistol for she'd stole away me rapier
But I couldn't shoot the water, so a prisoner I was taken.

[5]

If anyone can aid me 'tis me brother in the army.
If I can find his station be it in Cork or in Killarney
And if he's come and join me, we'd go rovin' in Kilkenny
And I'm sure he'll treat me better than me darlin' sporting
Jenny.

[6]

Now there's some take delight in the carriages a rolling,
And others take delight in the hurling and the bowling,
But I take delight in the juice of the barley,
And courting pretty fair maids in the morning bright and early.

The Holy Ground *(traditional)*

In the port town of Cobh (pronouned "cove"), firsherman
lived in a section of the town know as "The Holy Ground."
Despite it's reverent sound, the Holy Ground was actually the
city's red light district.

"The Holy Ground" is a type of sea shanty called a *capstan
shanty*. The capstan is a manual machine on sailing vessels
into which wooden lever are placed. Sailors push the levers to
apply tension to ropes to hoist sails and raise anchors. As the
capstan was pushed, sailors would sing songs to coordinate
their movements.

[Chorus]

C   **Am F G**

You're the girl that I do adore,

 F   **Am**

And still I live in hope to see

  C **G7**   **C**

The Holy Ground once more.

   C   **G7** **C**   **G** **C**

Fare thee well my lovely darlin', a thousand times adieu!

      Am   **F** **G**   **C**

For we're sailing away from the Holy Ground, and the girls

   G7

we all love true.

    C   **G**   **C**   **Am**   **F G**

We will sail the salt seas over, and then return for shore,

 F   **Am**   **C** **G7**

To see again the girls we love, and the Holy Ground once

 C

more.

A model of a capstan in action, perhaps with the sailors singing "The Holy Ground"

[2]

And now the storm is raging, and we are far from shore
And the good old ship is tossing about, and the rigging is all
tore
And the secret of my life, my love, you're the girl that I adore
But still I live in hope to see, Holy Ground once more.
FINE GIRL, YOU ARE!

[3]

And now the storm is over, and we are safe and well
We will go down to a public house, and we'll sit and drink
our fill.
We will drink strong ale and porter, and we'll make the rafters
roar,
And when all our money is spent, we will go to sea once
more! FINE GIRL, YOU ARE!

The Rock of Cashel

The Rock of Cashel is one Ireland's greatest treasures. With ties to St. Patrick and Brian Boru, as well Pagan chieftains of the pre-Christian era, Cashel represents an unparalleled span of Irish history. From the Gaelic word "caiseal" meaning "stone fort," Cashel has been a fortified place since the forth century. The Kings of Munster, beginning with Conall Corc in 370 AD, ruled for over 600 years.

In 453 AD, St. Patrick personally converted Aengus MacMut Fraich, the third King of Munster, to Christianity. Brian Boruma mac Cennetig (Brian Boru), Ireland's most famous king, was crowned here in 976 AD. He successfully united Ireland, becoming High King in 1002. At the Battle of Clontarf, near Dublin, Brian succeeded in ending Viking domination of Ireland in 1014. In the late 1200s, King Muircheartac O'Brien deeded the Rock of Cashel to the Roman Catholic Bishop of Limerick. It was used by the Catholic Church and then the Church of Ireland until it was sacked by Oliver Cromwell's forces in 1649.

ON THE WAY FROM CORK TO DUBLIN

On the much traveled road from Cork to Dublin, you will have much to see and sing about. All three songs included here meet with tragic consequences, but your spirits will be buoyed with a side trip to the breathtakingly beautiful sights of Glendalough Abbey in the Wicklow mountains.

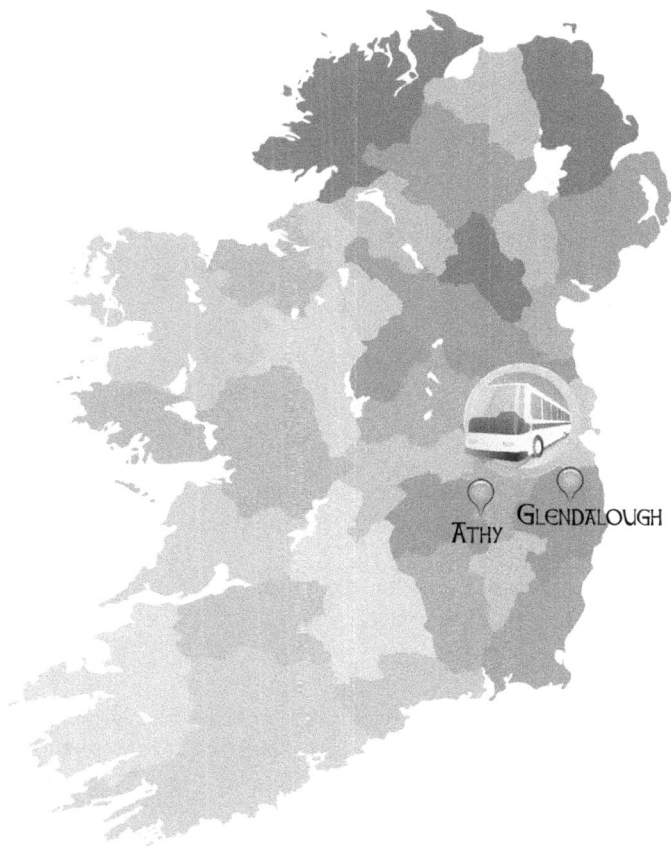

JOHNNY, I HARDLY KNEW YE *(Geoghegan, traditional)*

Sung to the tune of "When Johnny Comes Marching Home" and originally believed to have been an Irish anti-recruiting lyric written in the late eighteenth century, the words to "Johnny, I Hardly Knew Ye" may actually have been written by an Englishman and music hall songwriter, Joseph B. Geoghegan, in 1867. It tells the story of a Irish woman who later meets the lover who deserted her and their illegitimate child by running off to war. The song is set to a traditional air.

Em   **G**
While going the road to sweet Athy, har-oo, ha-roo,
    Em   **G**   **B7**
While going the road to sweet Athy, har-oo, har-oo,
    Em   **D**
While going the road to sweet Athy,
 C   **B7**
A stick in my hand and a tear in my eye,
   Em   **D**   **C**   **B7**
A doleful damsel I heard cry,
Em
Johnny, I hardly knew ye...

[Chorus]
With drums and guns and guns and drums, ha-roo, ha-roo,
With drums and guns and guns and drums, ha-roo, ha-roo,
With drums and guns and guns and drums
The enemy nearly slew ye,
My Johnny dear, you look so queer,
Johnny, I hardly knew ye.

[2]
Where are the eyes that looked so mild, ha-roo, haroo,
Where are the eyes that looked so mild, ha-roo, ha-roo,
Where are the eyes that looked so mild,

When my poor heart you first beguiled,
Why did you skedaddle from me and the child,
Johnny, I hardly knew ye.

[3]

Where are the legs with which you run, ha-roo, ha-roo
Where are the legs with which you run, ha-roo, ha-roo
Where are the legs with which you run,
When you went to shoulder a gun,
Indeed your dancing days are done.
Johnny, I hardly knew ye.

[4]

You haven't an arm and you haven't a leg, haroo, ha-roo
You haven't an arm and you haven't a leg, ha-roo, haroo
You haven't an arm and you haven't a leg,
You're an eyeless, noseless, chicken-less egg,
You'll have to be put in a bowl to beg,
Johnny, I hardly knew ye.

Pictured above is Dublin Castle, the seat of British rule in Ireland throughout the nineteenth century until 1922. During World War I, a section of Dublin Castle was converted into a military hospital for wounded troops in the British Army.

Rocky Road to Dublin *(Gavan, traditional)*

This is a fast tempo nineteenth century song written for the English music hall scene tells the sad tale of an Irishman who leaves his home in Tuam, Ireland, bound for Liverpool by way of Dublin. Along the way, he is mocked, robbed, beaten, and eventually rescued by Irishmen from Galway.

Am
In the merry month of May from my home I started
               G
Left the girls of Tuam nearly broken-hearted
Am
Saluted Father dear, kissed my darlin' Mother
                   G
Drank a pint of beer my grief and tears to smother
Am   **C**   **Am**   **C**
Then off to reap the corn, and leave where I was born
Am   **C**   **G**
I cut a stout blackthorn to banish ghosts and goblins
Am   **C**   **Am**   **C**
In a bran' new pair of brogues rattling o'er the bogs
Am   **G**
And frightened all the dogs on the rocky road to Dublin.

[Chorus]
One, two, three, four five,

Am
Hunt the hare and turn her down the rocky road,
G   **Am**
And all the way to Dublin. Whack fol-lol-de ra.

[2]
In Mullingar that night, I rested limbs so weary,
Started by daylight next morning light and airy,
Took a drop of the pure, to keep my heart from sinking,
That's an Irishman's cure, whene'er he's on for drinking,

To see the lasses smile, laughing all the while,
At my curious style. 'twould set your heart a-bubbling,
They ax'd if I was hired, the wages I required,
Till I was almost tired of the rocky road to Dublin.

[3]

In Dublin next arrived, I thought it such a pity,
To be so soon deprived a view of that fine city,
Then I took a stroll out among the quality,
My bundle it was stole in a neat locality;
Something crossed my mind, then I looked behind,
No bundle could I find upon me stick a-wobblin',
Enquiring for the rogue, they said my Connaught brogue
Wasn't much in vogue on the rocky road to Dublin.

[4]

From there I got away my spirits never failing,
Landed on the quay as the ship was sailing,
Captain at me roared, said that no room had he,
When I jumped aboard, a cabin found for Paddy
Down among the pigs, I played some funny rigs
Danced some hearty jigs, the water round me bubblin'
When off to Holyhead I wished myself was dead,
Or better far, instead, on the rocky road to Dublin.

[5]

The boys of Liverpool, when we safely landed,
Called myself a fool, I could no longer stand it;
Blood began to boil, temper I was losin'
Poor old Erin's isle they began abusin'
"Hurrah my soul!" sez I, my shillelagh I let fly,
Some Galway boys were by, saw I was a hobble in,
Then with a loud Hurrah, they joined in the affray,
We quickly cleared the way, for the rocky road to Dublin.

GLENDALOUGH SAINT *(traditional)*

The "Glendalough Saint" was Saint Kevin, who founded the Abbey of Glendalough in County Wicklow in the sixth century. He was known to be very kind to animals but not so fond of people. Local St. Kevin lore mentions that he managed to keep is community well fed with a bounty of fish that were brought to him by a friendly otter.

The song tells the story of a young woman named Kathleen, who fell in love with Saint Kevin and offered him a wide range of womanly services, from cleaner to bed warmer. It is said that Kevin would have nothing to do with her, so he beat her with stinging nettles to chase her off. When she returned undeterred, he pushed her out of his cave and into the lake and she immediately drowned.

D
In Glendalough lived an old saint
                           A
Renowned for learning and piety
D   **G**
His manners was curious and quaint
       A   **D**
And he looked upon girl with disparity

[Chorus]
Fol di dol fol di fol day,
Fol di dol rol di dol ad dy,
Fol di dol rol di dol day,
Fol di dol rol di dol ad dy.

[2]
He was fond of readin' a book
When he could get one to his wishes
He was fond of castin' his hook
In among the ould fishes.

46

[3]

But one evenin' he landed a trout,

He landed a fine big rout, Sir.

When young Kathleen from over the way

Came to see what the ould monk was about, sir.

[4]

"Oh get out o' me way" said the saint,

"For I am a man of great piety

"And me good manners I wouldn't taint

"Not by mixing with female society."

St. Kevin's Church,
Glendalough

[5]

Oh but Kitty she wouldn't give in

And when he got home to his rockery,

He found she was seated therein

A-polishin' up his ould crockery.

[6]

Well he gave the poor creature a shake

And I wish that the Garda had caught him

For he threw her right into the lake

And, be Jaysus, she sank to the bottom.

Monasticism

Monasticism came to Ireland in the fifth century. Early examples of monasteries include St. Caillan in County Leitrim (ca. 500s) and Inisbofin on the Island of Loughree (ca. 540). Many of Patrick's converts embraced monasticism but it was not until after his death that it took off. By 650 at least a hundred monasteries had been established across Ireland. Glendalough, established by St. Kevin in about 600, flourished for 600 years before succumbing to Norman invaders in 1214. Monasteries rose in wealth and power, and became great centers of learning. They perfected the scribal art with its unique illuminative style, made famous by the *Book of Kells*, of copying scripture. One of Christianity's greatest contributions to the Irish was the application of the written word to ancient Irish oral traditions.

Page from the Book of Kells

DUBLIN

We continue our musical voyage across Ireland as we enter
Eire's capitol city. Dublin is a center for culture and the arts
and has produced some of the world's best writers and
songwriters. Included in this section, however, are songs that
provide a slice of Dublin's ordinary life, from fishmongers, to
red light districts, to prisons, and to the problem of finding
affordable housing.

DUBLIN

When you're in Dublin, be sure to visit the Molly
Malone statue on Grafton Street. Built by Jeanne
Rynhart to commemorate the capitol city's millenial
celebration in 1988, the almost life-sized bronze statue is
know affectionately to locals as the "tart with the cart."

MOLLY MALONE *(traditional)*

Also known as "Cockles and Mussels," "Molly Malone" is
Dublin's unofficial anthem. It shares the story of a young
Dublin fishmonger who continued to work even after death.

[Chorus]
"Alive, alive, Oh! Alive, alive Oh!".
Crying "Cockles and mussels, alive, alive oh!"

    C   **Am**   **Dm**   **G7**
In Dublin's fair city, where the girls are so pretty,
   C   **A7**   **D7**   **G7**
I first set my eyes on sweet Molly Malone,
          C   **Am**
As she wheeled her wheel barrow
      Dm   **G7**
Through streets broad and narrow
      C   **Gm**   **Am** **G** **C**
Crying "Cockles and mussels, alive, alive-oh!"

[2]
She was a fishmonger and sure 'twas no wonder
For so was her father and mother before.
And they both wheeled their barrows
Through streets broad and narrow,
Crying "Cockles and mussels, alive, alive-oh!"

[3]
She died of a fever and no one could save her,
And that was the end of sweet Molly Malone.
Now her ghost wheels her barrow
Through streets broad and narrow,
Crying "Cockles and mussels, alive, alive-oh!"

MONTO *(George Desmond Hodnett)*

A music critic for the *Irish Times*, George Desmond Hodnett, wrote "Monto" in 1958 and never intended for it to be performed publicly. When The Dubliners sang it in a recorded concert performance at the Gate Theatre in 1966, however, it became an immediate national hit.

Monto is the nickname for Montgomery Street, an area that was once one of Dublin's hottest red light districts. Many famous writers, politicians, and even royalty spent a bit of recreation time in Monto in the late nineteenth century.

    F   **Dm**   **F**   **Dm**
Well if you got a wing-o, take her up to Ring-o,
    F   **Dm**   **F C F**
Where the waxies sing-o, all the day.
        F   **Dm**   **F**   **Dm**
If you've had your fill of porter and you can't go any further,
    F   **Dm**   **F C**   **F**
Give your man the order, "Back to the Quay!"
    F   **Dm** **F**   **Dm**
And take her up to Monto, Monto, Monto,
    F   **Dm**   **F C F C F**
Take her up to Monto, lan-ge- roo. To you!

[2]
Have you heard of Buckshot Forster, the dirty old impostor,
Took a mot and lost her, up the Furry Glen.
He first put on his bowler and buttoned up his trousers,
Then whistled for a growler and he said, "My man!"
Take me up to Monto, Monto, Monto,
Take me up to Monto, lan-ge- roo. To you!

[3]
When Carey told on Skin-the-goat, O'Donnell caught him on the boat,
He wished he'd never been afloat, the dirty skite.

For it wasn't very sensible to tell on the Invincibles,
They stuck up for their principles, day and night.
Be going up to Monto, Monto, Monto,
Be going up to Monto, lan-ge- roo. To you!

[4]

You've seen the Dublin Fusiliers, the dirty old
bamboozeleers,
They went and got their childer, one, two, three.
Marching from the Linen Hall, there's one for every
cannonball,
And Vicky's going to send them all, o'er the sea.
They first went up to Monto, Monto, Monto,
They first went up to Monto, lan-ge- roo. To you!

[5]

Now when the Tsar of Russia and the King of Prussia
Landed in the Phoenix in a big balloon.
They asked the police band to play "The Wearin' of the
Green"
But the buggers from the depot didn't know the tune.
So they all went up to Monto, Monto, Monto,
They all went up to Monto, lan-ge- roo. To you!

[6]

The Queen she came to call on us, she wanted to see all of
us,
I'm glad she didn't fall on us, she's eighteen stone.
"Mister Me Lord Mayor," says she, "Is this all you've got to
show me?"
"Why, no ma'am there's some more to see, Póg mo thóin!"
And he took her up Monto, Monto, Monto,
He took her up in Monto, lan-ge- roo. To you!

DICEY REILLY *(traditional)*

From the other characters mentioned in "Dicey Reilly," it can be surmised that Miss Dicey Reilly was employed in the "hospitality trade" down in the red-light district of Monto. Both Becky Cooper and May Oblong were both infamous Dublin madams in the early 20th century. Dicey Reilly, however, was the "heart of rowl," an old Dublin expression for the best quality of leaves at the center of a roll of tobacco. This meant that ol' Dicey was genuine and of the best quality, despite her profession and taking to the sup.

[Chorus]

  G   **D**   **G**
Poor old Dicey Reilly, she has taken to the sup.
  D   **G**
Poor old Dicey Reilly, she will never give it up.
        G
For it's off each morning to the hop
  D
She goes in for another little drop,
  G   **D G**
For the heart of the rowl is Dicey Reilly.

[2]

She walks along Fitzgibbon Street
With an independent air,
Down along by Summerhill
At her, the people stare,
She says, "It's nearly half past one,
"Time I went in for another little one,"
For the heart of the rowl is Dicey Reilly.

Street sign for Fitzgibbon Street in Dublin. Unlike cities in the U.S., Dublin's street signs are not placed on signposts but are instead located on buildings at the corner of street junctions. The signs typically list both the English and Irish names of the street and the area's postal code number.

[3]

She owns a little sweet shop
At the corner of the street
And every evening after school,
I go to wash her feet.
She'd leave me there to mind the shop,
She goes in for another little drop,
For the heart of the rowl is Dicey Reilly

[4]

In days of old when men were men
And they fancied May Oblong,
Lovely Beckie Cooper now
Or Maggie Mary Wong.
One girl put them all to shame,
One was worthy of the name,
And the name of the same was Dicey Reilly.

55

KIMMAGE *(unknown)*

Kimmage is a working class suburb of Dublin and is one of the two chest properties in the Irish version of Monopoly. Although the origins and age of the song are debated, many Dubs (people from Dublin) love it because of the fun picture it paints of everyday life in twentieth century Ireland.

D
There were three lovely lasses from Kimmage,
      A7   **D**
From Kimmage, from Kimmage
D
And when ever there's a bit of a scrimmage,
   G   **A7**   **D**
Sure I was the toughest of all
 G   **A7**   **D**
Sure I was the toughest of all.

[2]
Now the cause of the row was Joe Cashin,

Joe Cashin, Joe Cashin,

For he told me he thought I looked smashing

At a dance in the Adelaide hall.

At a dance in the Adelaide hall.

[3]
When he gets a few jars he goes frantic,

Oh frantic, oh frantic

But he's tall and he's dark and romantic

And I love him in spite of it all.

And I love him in spite of it all.

[4]
Now the other two young ones were flippin',

Were flippin',were flippin',

When they saw me and Joe were trippin',
To the strains of the Tennessee waltz.
To the strains of the Tennessee waltz.

[5]

Now he told me he thought we should marry,
Should marry, should marry,
For he said I was foolish to tarry,
So I lent him the price of the ring.
So I lent him the price of the ring.

[6]

Now me da said he'll give us a present,
A present, a present,
An oul' stool and a lovely stuffed pheasant
And a picture to hang on the wall.
And a picture to hang on the wall.

[7]

I went down to the tenancy section,
The section, the section,
The T.D. before the election
Said he'd get me a house near me ma.
Said he'd get me a house near me ma.

[8]

Well we're getting the house the man said it,
He said it, he said it
When I've five or six kids to me credit,
In the meantime we'll live with me ma.
In the meantime we'll live with me ma.

SPANISH LADY *(traditional)*

This traditional tune, with lyrics of unknown origins, dates back to the eighteenth century and is about a man who never forgot a chance encounter with an alluring Spanish lady.

G		Em		C		D

G   **Em**   **C**   **D**
As I went down through Dublin City at the hour of twelve in the night
G   **Em**   **C**   **D**
Who should I see but a Spanish Lady washing her feet by candle light
G   **Em**   **G**   **Am**   **D**
First she washed them, then she dried them over a fire of amber coal
G   **Em**   **C**   **D**
In all my life I ne'er did see a maid so sweet about the soul.

[Chorus]

Whack for the too-ra-loo-ra-laddy, whack for the too-ra-loo-ra-lay,
Whack for the too-ra-loo-ra-laddy, whack for the too-ra-loo-ra-lay.

[2]

As I came back through Dublin City at the hour of half past eight,
Who should I spy but the Spanish Lady brushing her hair in the broad daylight.
First she tossed it, then she brushed it, on her lap was a silver comb.
In all my life I ne'er did see, a maid so fair since I did roam.

[3]

As I went back through Dublin City as the sun began to set
Who should I spy but the Spanish Lady catching a moth in a golden net.
When she saw me, then she fled me lifting her petticoat over her knees.
In all my life I ne'er did see a maid so shy as the Spanish Lady.

[4]

I've wandered north and I've wandered south through Stonybatter and Patrick's close,
Up and around by the Gloucester Diamond and back by Napper Tandy's house.
Old age has laid her hand on me cold as a fire of ashy coals.
In all my life I ne'er did see a maid so sweet as the Spanish Lady.

MICK THE MOAN *(Philip M. Price)*

In Irish English, to "moan" is to complain about something.
Philip Price wrote this song many years ago for one of his
friends who was a chronic complainer, Mick the Moan, to
sing on his wedding day.

D
Me and me mates we battled through blood,
Always in sorrow could see only good,
But one weekend as far away we did roam,
A   **G**   **D**
Joe Byrne, he introduced Mick the Moan.

[Chorus]
G   **D**
With "The waters too wet," "The waters too dry,"
A
"The sun shouldn't be so high in the sky!"
D
I really rue the day that I got a new phone
A
For I'm always the first to hear Mick's new moan.

[2]
When we go camping, we liked to look rough
Do all the things that would make us real tough.
But Mick brings a suitcase, pajamas, and comb
And spends all the day making up new moans.

[3]
Mick went to the Blood Bank one day,
He went to give a pint of his blood away.
They always give a pencil saying, "The owner is a donor,"
But they wrote on Mick's pencil, "The owner is a moaner."

[4]

They say that when a Dub takes a woman for his wife,
She's going to end up nagging him the rest of his life.
But poor old Anne won't even get in a groan,
I hear she's marrying Mick the Moan.

Philip heard many of Mick's old and new moans over pints of Guinness at
O'Donoghue's Pub near St. Stephen's Green in Dublin. O'Donoghue's is a
fixture in the traditional Irish music scene. Many famous Irish singers and
musicians have played there over the years, including The Dubliners, Christy
Moore, Joe Heany, Phil Lynott, Seamus Ennis, and The Fureys.

It's worth a visit to pop in for a pint because you can often find a music session
going on and the walls are a treasure trove of Irish music, lined with photos of
all those who have played there. There's even a photo of Bruce Springsteen!

The Vikings

The first Viking raid on Ireland was at the monastery on Rathlin Island off the north coast in 795. Eighth century Ireland was a rural, agrarian society with hundreds of tiny fractious kingdoms and no central power to rally a fighting force. After nearly 50 years of coastal raids Vikings began establishing forts along the coast of Ireland. By 850, these included forts at Dublin, Waterford, and Cork on the east coast; and Shannon and Limerick on the west coast. Viking raiders sought booty and slaves and these forts enabled them to conduct raids further inland in search of both.

Giving up their seaborne hit and run tactics for land based raids made them easy targets for Irish kings seeking revenge. In 1014, Brian Boru united the Irish in the successful Battle of Clontarf against the Dublin Vikings, beginning the decline of Viking power in Ireland.

Like the Vikings, the Rogues & Wenches have similarly raided Ireland's shores in search of booty

THE NORTH

Although part of the Emerald Isle, Northern Ireland has for many years been part of the United Kingdom. Despite the area's colorful history, it shares a common culture and love of traditional music with the rest of Ireland.

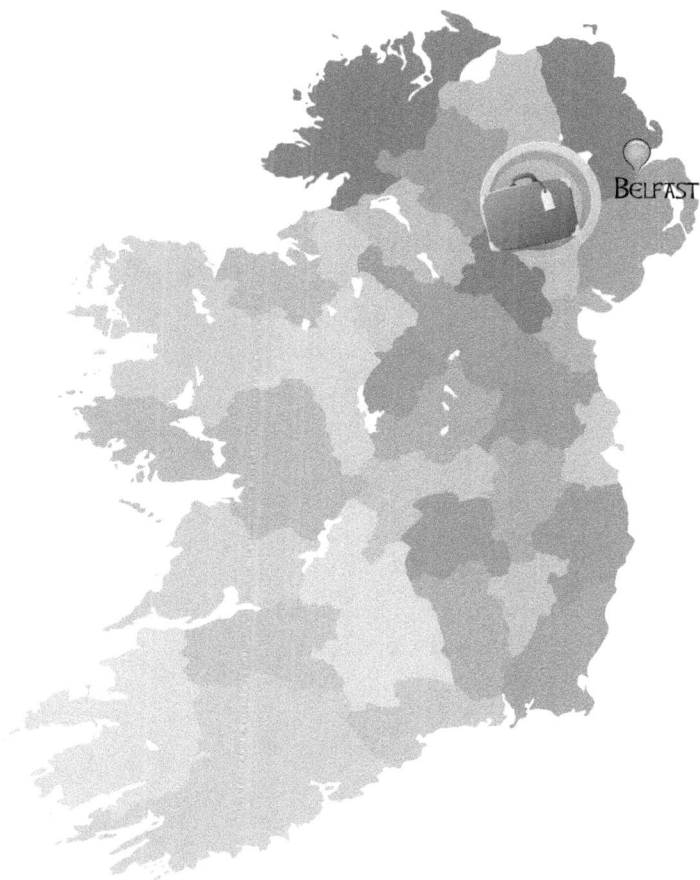

BELFAST

BLACK VELVET BAND *(traditional)*

This traditional Irish song from the nineteenth century describes the common practice of *transportation*, a common punishment used to send criminals, even the pettiest of criminals, to be transported to the Australian penal colony on the island of Tasmania, also known as Van Diemen's Land.

D
In a neat little town they call Belfast
                                 A
Apprenticed to trade I was bound
D   **Bm**
And many an hour's sweet happiness
G   **A**   **D**
I spent in that neat little town.

Till bad misfortune came o'er me
That caused me to stray from the land
Far away from my friends and relations
To follow the black velvet band.

[Chorus]
Her eyes they shone like the diamonds.
You'd think she was queen of the land
And her hair hung over her shoulder,
Tied up with a black velvet band.

[2]
Well, I was out strolling one evening,
Not meaning to go very far
When I met with a pretty young damsel
Who was selling her trade in the bar.
When a gold watch, she took from a customer
And slipped it right into my hand

Then the Watch came and put me in prison
Bad luck to the black velvet band.

[3]
Next morning before judge and jury,
For a trial I had to appear,
And the judge, he said, "You young fellows...
"The case against you is quite clear.
"And seven long years is your sentence.
"You're going to Van Dieman's Land
"Far away from your friends and relations
"To follow the black velvet band."

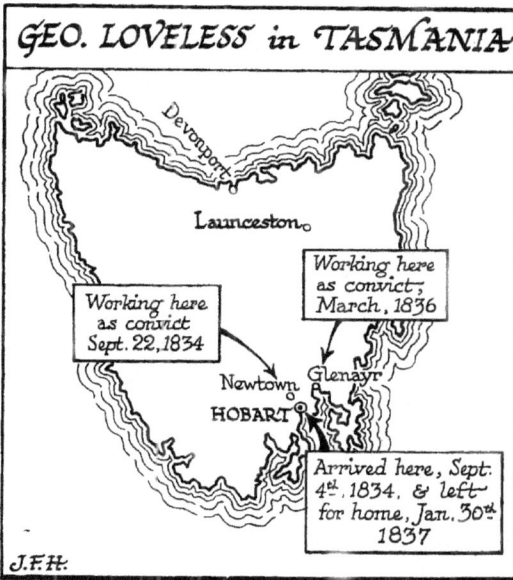

GEO. LOVELESS in TASMANIA

Devonport

Launceston

Working here as convict, March, 1836

Working here as convict Sept. 22, 1834

Newtown   Glenayr
HOBART

Arrived here, Sept. 4th, 1834, & left for home, Jan. 30th 1837

J.F.H.

Unlike the narrator of "The Black Velvet Band," who was unknowingly involved in an actual crime, many living under British rule were sent to Australian penal colonies for acts that would not be considered criminal today. Pictured above is a map of George Loveless' time as a Tasmanian convict. Loveless was taken from his farm in Tolpuddle, England and sent to Tasmania with out his family's knowledge for setting up a small farmers' trade union.

Tell Me Ma *(traditional)*

It is a popular traditional children's song that traveled with the Irish around the world, with the original "Belfast city" lyrics changing to Dublin in Ireland, London in England, Edinburgh in Scotland, and Brisbane in Australia.

When sung by children in Ireland, they join hands and form a circle, with one child in the middle. When the chorus verse finishes, the child in the middle says the initials of another child playing the game, who then replaces them in the center of the circle.

    G
I'll tell me ma when I go home,
       D   **G**
Well the boys won't leave the girls alone.
  G
Pull on me hair and they stole my comb,
D   **G**
That's all right till I go home.

[Chorus]
 G   **C**
She is handsome, she is pretty,
G   **D**
She is the belle of Belfast city,
G   **C**
She is courting one, two, three,
G   **D**   **G**
Please, won't you tell me, who is she.

[2]
Albert Mooney said he loves her,
All the boys are fighting for her,
Knock on the door, and they ring on the bell,
Oh my true love, are you well.

[3]

Out she comes as white as snow,

Rings on her fingers and bells on her toes,

Old Johhny Murphy says she'll die,

When she doesn't get the guy with the roving eye.

[4]

Let the wind and the rain and the hail blow high,

Snow come tumbling from the sky,

She's as sweet as an apple pie,

She'll get her own lad by and by.

[5]

When she gets a lad of her own,

She won't tell her ma when she gets home,

Let them all come as they will,

For it's Albert Mooney she loves still.

Philip M. Price in a typical early nineteenth century Irish countryside home

Saint Patrick

Separating the mythical Saint Patrick from the historical St. Patrick is not easy. Mythical St. Patrick single handedly converted all of Ireland to Christianity, banished the snakes, and explained the idea of the Holy Trinity using a shamrock. Historical St. Patrick arrived in Ireland in about 435. He was from the west coast of Roman Britain. His father was a town councilor and a deacon and his grandfather a priest.

At the age of 16, Patrick was captured by Irish raiders and enslaved in Ireland for six years. It is unclear if he escaped or was released but upon his return he received formal training in the priesthood. He worked primarily in the north of Ireland establishing his see at Armagh, the seat of Ireland's most powerful king at the time. From here he set out on his missionary journeys. By the time of his death in ca. 460 Christianity had a solid footing in Ireland.

THE HIGH SEAS

With a couple of Rogues & Wenches as coauthors of this book, you know we can't stay on dry land too long! In this section are a few favorite sea shanties and pirate songs sung by both the Rogues & Wenches and Philip Price.

ROLLING HOME *(Charles MacKay, traditional)*

"Rolling Home" is a homeward-bound, capstan shanty set to a traditional air, with the lyrics from a 19th century poem by Charles MacKay. Although many European counties claim timeless shanty as their own, with the lyrics slightly varied from country to country, the Rogues & Wenches sing the lyrics below, taken from the Scots group Old Blind Dogs.

[Chorus]
Rolling home, rolling home,
Rolling home, across the sea.
Rolling home to Caledonia,
Rolling home, dear land, to thee.

     G
Call all hands to man the capstan.
         G7   **C**
See the cable running clear.
     D   **G**
Heave around and with the wheel, boys,
     D   **G**
For our homeland we must steer.

[2]
From the pines of California,
And by Chile's endless strand
We have sailed the world twice over,
Every port in every land.

[3]
And to all ye blaggard pirates,
Who would chase us from the waves,
Heed ye well that those who've tried us
Soon have found their watery graves!

The Rogues & Wenches rolling home to the
Salty Dog Saloon in Homer, Alaska

[4]

We were boarded in Jamaica
Where the Jolly Roger flew.
But our swords were hardly drawn, boys,
Ere they took a rosy hue.

[5]

We return with precious cargo,
And with bounty coined in gold.
And our sweethearts will rejoice, boys,
For they love their sailors bold.

JOLLY ROVING TAR *(traditional)*

This song is sung by the Great Big Sea, one of the favorite groups of the Rogues & Wenches. Just like the Great Big Sea, "Jolly Roving Tar" hails from Newfoundland, a Canadian province with strong Irish roots. It is rumored that Erin of the Rogues & Wenches is in love with the Great Big Sea's lead singer, Alan Doyle. Should you ever meet Mr. Doyle, be sure to mention Erin to him!

[Chorus]
When your money's all gone, it's the same old song.

"Get up, Jack! John, sit down!"

Come along, come along, ye jolly brave boys,

There's lots of grog in the jar.

We'll plough the briny ocean with the jolly roving tar.

D   G   A   D

Ships may come and ships may go, as long as the sea does roll.

            G   A   D

Each sailor lad, just like his dad; he loves a flowing bowl.

            G   D   A

A trip ashore, he does adore, with a girl that's plump and round.

[2]
When Jack gets in, it's then he'll steer

For some old boarding house.

They'll welcome him with rum and gin;

They'll feed him on pork scouse.

He'll lend and spend and not offend,

Till he lies drunk on the ground.

[3]
He then will sail aboard some ship

For India or Japan.

In Asia fair the ladies there

All love a sailor man.
He'll go ashore and on a tear,
He'll buy some girl a gown.

[4]
When Jack gets old and weather-beat,
Too old to roam about,
In some rum shop, they'll let him stop,
Till eight bells calls him out.
He'll raise his eyes up to the skies,
Sayin', "Boys, we're homeward bound!"

Signal Hill on the coast of St. John's, Newfoundland

More than one fifth of all "Newfies," as people from Newfoundland are called, are of Irish descent. Trading ships came from County Cork to the shores of Newfoundland as early as 1536 and the island's connection to Eire hasn't stopped since. Irish music is very popular on the island province and many Newfies have an accent that is almost indistinguishable from an Irish accent.

73

SOUTH AUSTRALIA *(traditional)*

"South Australia" is a rousing sea shanty with a call and response, a popular technique in sea shanties in which one voice calls out a phrase and another voice or set of voices responds. It was also a work song heard on the merchant clipper ships transporting goods between Australia and London.

[Chorus]

G   D
Haul away you rolling king,
G   D   G   D
Heave away! Haul away!
G   D
All the way you'll hear me sing,
                  A   D
And we're bound for South Australia!

      D   G   D
In South Australia I was born
G   D   G   D
Heave away! Haul away!
               A   D
South Australia round Cape Horn.
               A   D
And we're bound for South Australia!

[2]

As I walked out one morning fair,
Heave away! Haul away!
It's there I met Miss Nancy Blair,
And we're bound for South Australia!

[3]

There ain't but one thing grieves my mind,
Heave away! Haul away!
It's to leave Miss Nancy Blair behind,
And we're bound for South Australia!

[4]

I run her all night; I run her all day.
Heave away! Haul away!
Run her before we sailed away.
And we're bound for South Australia!

[5]

I shook her up; I shook her down.
Heave away! Haul away!
I shook her round and round and round,
And we're bound for South Australia!

[6]

And as you wallop round Cape Horn.
Heave away! Haul away!
You'll wish that you had never been born.
And we're bound for South Australia!

[7]

I wish I was on Australia's strand.
Heave away! Haul away!
With a bottle of whiskey in my hand,
And we're bound for South Australia!

Mingulay Boat Song *(Hugh Roberton, traditional)*

The lyrics to "Mingulay Boat Song" were written by Sir Hugh S. Roberton in the 1930s, but the tune was a traditional Gaelic one. The song celebrates the inhabitants of Mingulay, an island in the cold waters of Scotland's outer Hebrides, which was continuously inhabited from the days of the Iron Age until its last residents left in 1912.

This was one of the first songs the Rogues & Wenches sang as a band and it has become a concert staple for the group. They often open with their evening concerts with a signature arrangement of "Mingulay."

[Chorus]
Heel y'ho, boys, let her go, boys!
Heave her head 'round to the weather!
Heel y'ho, boys, let her go, boys!
Sailing homeward to Mingulay!

       D
What care we how white the Minch is?
    A   **G**
What care we for wind or weather?
    D
For we know that every inch is
    A   **D**
Sailing closer to Mingulay!

[2]
Wives are waiting on the banks or
Gazing seaward from the heather.
Heave her 'round, boys, and we'll anchor
Ere the sun sets on Mingulay.

[3]
When the wind is wild with shouting,

And the waves mount ever higher,
Anxious eyes turn ever seaward
To see you home, boys, to Mingulay.

[4]
Far behind us hills of Quinlon.
Soon before us hills of heather.
And you know boys, candles glow, boys,
In the windows of Mingulay.

*The Rogues & Wenches in Alaska's own
highlands in Hatcher Pass*

Haul Away Joe *(traditional)*

During the eighteenth and nineteenth, his sea shanty was popular among sailors on British ships, many of whom were Irish.

Am   **Em**
When I was a wee young lad
Dm   **Am**
Twas then me mother told me, Timmy!
Way, haul away, we'll haul away, Joe!
That if I did not kiss the gals
Me lips would all grow moldy, Timmy!
Way, haul away, we'll haul away, Joe!

[Chorus]
Way, haul away, were bound for rougher weather Timmy
Way, haul away, we'll haul away, Joe!

[2]
King Louis was the king of France
Before the revolution...Timmy!
Way, haul away, we'll haul away, Joe!
But then he got his head cut off
Which spoiled his constitution...Timmy!
Way, haul away, we'll haul away, Joe!

[3]
The first I met was an Yankee lass
Now she was fat and lazy, Timmy!
Way haul away we'll haul away joe.
Next I met was an Irish Lass she nearly drove me crazy
Way haul away, we'll haul away Joe.Timmy!

[4]

The cook is in the galley boys
Making duff so handy, Timmy
Way, haul away, we'll haul away, Joe!
The captain's in his cabin lads
Drinking wine and brandy, Timmy
Way, haul away, we'll haul away, Joe!

No trip is complete without sampling the local cuisine. In Ireland, the one food that you must try if you try no other is fish and chips. Although first made popular in England, fish and chips became standard fare for Irish families on a Friday night because the only meat allowed by the Catholic Church on Fridays was fish.

Every town has their favorite "chippers" or fish and chip shop. Some are sit down restaurants, like the chipper on Inishmore pictured above, while others are entirely take-away, like Dublin's wildly popular chipper, Leo Burdock's.

SPANISH LADIES *(traditional)*

"Spanish Ladies" is an 18th century navy song that was also sung by merchant sailors. From 1793 to 1796, British ships frequently docked in Spanish harbors, allowing sailors to encounter many a Spanish Lady.

[Chorus]
We'll rant and we'll roar like true English sailors.
We'll rant and we'll roar along the salt sea,
Until we strike soundings in the channel of old England.
From Ushant to Scilly be thirty-five leagues.

```
  Em              G              D
Farewell and adieu, to you Spanish ladies
  Em                        G              D
Farewell and adieu, to you daughters of Spain
   Em            D     C          Em
For we've received orders to sail for old England,
   Em         D          C        Em
But we hope in short time to see you again.
```

[2]
Then we hove our ship to, with the wind at sou'west, boys.
We hove our ship to, for to strike soundings clear.
We filled the main topsail and bore right away, boys.
And straight up the channel of old England did steer.

[3]
Now the signal was made for the Grand fleet to anchor.
All on the Downs that night for to meet.
Then stand by your stoppers, see clear your shank-painters
Haul all your clew-garnets, stick out tacks and sheets.

[4]
Now let every man drink up his full bottle,
And let every man drink up his full glass.
We'll drink and be jolly and drown melancholy.
And here's to the health of each good-hearted lass.

Beyond Ireland's Shores

A song doesn't have to take place in Ireland to be an Irish song. Included in this section are songs about a group of Dublin tourists in the Isle of Man, Irish emigrants leaving Liverpool to head to America, and the beauty of Scotland written by a father and son from Belfast.

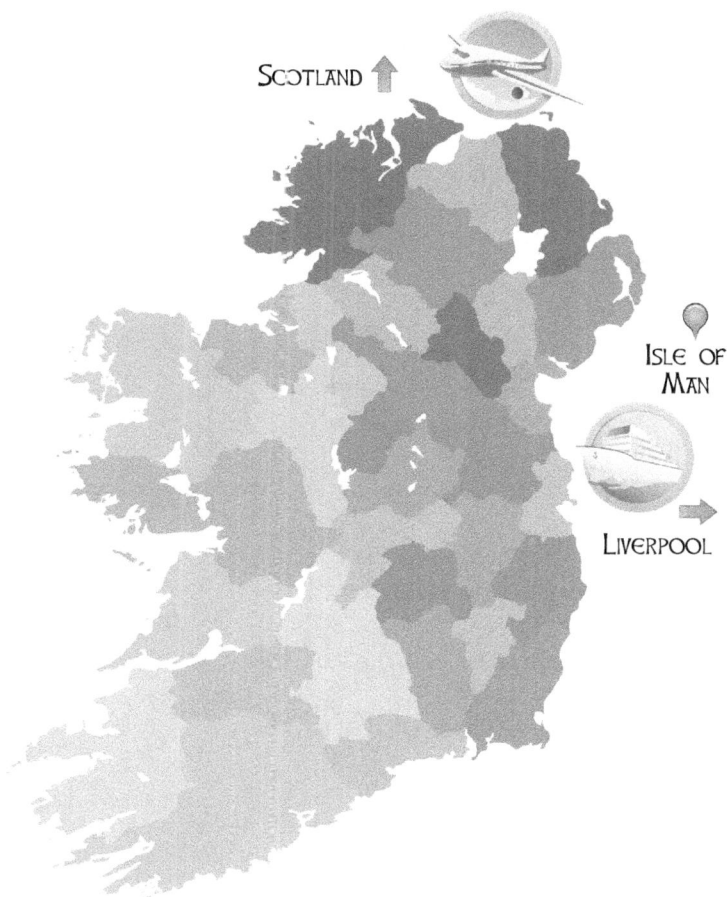

Scotland

Isle of Man

Liverpool

CRAIC WAS NINETY IN THE ISLE OF MAN

(Barney Rush)

The ferry from Dublin to the Isle of Man takes less than three hours, making it a popular destination for a weekend break from Dublin. Many make the trip for the *craic* (pronounced "crack") or good fun to be had on the island and in its pubs.

This classic Dublin song, written by Barney Rush, tells the story of how Barney and his mates went to the Isle of Man for a weekend and participated in a "ding dong," Dublin slang for a mighty music song session, even before the boat had left the Dublin port. As the song title suggests, the "craic was ninety," meaning the fun, music, singing, dancing, and drinking were great. However, Barney and his mates were not so lucky on this trip. They quickly got into women trouble, fight a few locals, land in jail, and get deported back to Ireland the next day.

G
Well, weren't we the rare aul stock,

Spent the evening getting locked,

D   **C**

In the Ace of Hearts, where the high stools were engaging.

G
Down by the Butt Bridge, down by the dock,

The boat she sailed at five o'clock.

D
"Hurry, lads," then said Whack,

      C

"Or before we're there we'll all be back.

      G

"Oh, carry him if you can."

        G   **D**   **G**

Oh the craic was ninety in the Isle of Man.

[2]

Before we reached the Alexander Base,
The ding dong we did surely raise,
In the bar of the ship well we had great sport,
As the boat sailed out from the port,
Landed up in the Douglas Head,
Enquiring for a vacant bed,
Got shown into the dining room,
By a decent woman up the road
Saying, "Ate up if ye can!"
Oh the craic was ninety in the Isle of Man.

[3]

Next morning went for a ramble round,
To see all the sights of Douglas Town,
Then we went for a mighty session,
In a pub they call Dick Darbys.
All got drunk by half past three,
To sober up, went swimmin' in the sea,
Back to the digs for the spruce up,
While waitin' for the Rosie,
We all drew up our plan.
Oh the craic was ninety in the Isle of Man.

[4]

That night we went to the Texas Bar,
We all came down by horse and car,
Met Big Jim and all went in
To drink some wine in Yates'.
The Liverpool Judies, it was said,
Were all to be found in the Douglas Head.
McShane was there with his tie and shirt,
The foreign girls he was tryin' to flirt.
Saying, "Here, girls, I'm your man,"
Oh the craic was ninety in the Isle of Man.

[5]

Whacker fancied his good looks
By an Isle of Man woman he was struck,
The Liverpool lad was by her side,
And he throwing the jar into her.
Whacker thought he'd take a chance,
He asked the quare one out to dance,
Around the floor they stepped it out,
To Whack it was no bother,
Well, everything goin' to plan.
Oh, the craic was ninety in the Isle of Man.

[6]

The Isle of Man woman fancied Whack,
Yer man waits there till his mates came back
Whack! They all whacked into Whack,
And Whack was landed on his back,
The police they arrived as well,
He landed a couple of them as well,
Spent the night in the Douglas jail,
Until the Dublin boat did sail,
Deported every man.
Oh, the craic was ninety in the Isle of Man.
Oh, the craic was ninety in the Isle of Man.

Philip sining "Craic Was Ninety in the Isle of Man" onboard the Mistral on the River Shannon

LEAVING OF LIVERPOOL *(traditional)*

"Leaving of Liverpool" is a traditional folk ballad in which the song's narrator leaves the port of Liverpool to emigrate to America.

This song is one of Rogues & Wenches' all time favorites. The band has very fond memories of a performance in which they sang "Leaving of Liverpool" while World Champion Irish Dancer Owen Barrington danced to the tune, with a synergy both infectious and irresistible.

[Chorus]
So fare thee well my own true love,
And when I return united we will be.
It's not the leaving of Liverpool that grieves me,
But my darling when I think of thee.

    D   **G**   **D**
Farewell to you my own true love,
                   A
I am going far, far away.
    D   **G**
I am bound for California,
      D   **A**   **D**
And I know that I'll return someday.

[2]
I have shipped on a Yankee sailing ship,
Davy Crocket is her name,
And Burgess is the captain of her
And they say she is a floating shame.

[3]
Oh, the sun is on the harbor love,
And I wish I could remain.
For I know it will be some long time
Before I see you again.

Saying Goodbye

Our musical journey across Ireland and beyond has come to a close. We end first with a poem called "St. Patrick's Mutton" to put you in the mood for St. Patrick's day. We end with our final song, "The Parting Glass," which is sung in pubs and homes across Ireland as friends and family depart for thee evening. In true Irish fashion, we must also end with a Irish blessing. This one is an original from Philip M. Price.

> *May you always have what you need,*
> *May you often get what you want,*
> *But may you not always get what you deserve.*

Weary travelers, from left to right: Philip M. Price, Robert Woofter, Lucia Woofter, and Darrell Lewis

St. Patrick's Mutton *a poem by Philip M. Price*

Let me tell you a bit of a story,
For it shows St Paddy in all his
blessed glory,
And also gives an explanation, long
overdue you say,
Why the Irish don't eat mutton on
St. Patricks day.

As you know he was stolen from
very far away,
And as a shepherd, he spent many a
cold night and day,
And diligent he was for he knew the
cost,
Of how he would get his arse kicked
if a single lamb was lost.

So there on the hill both night and
day,
He prayed, watched the flock, and
kept the wolf at bay,
But one winter's night to keep warm,
he drank a lot of tea
And his blessed bladder being small,
he found he had to wee.

Now blessed Paddy was very
blessed but was also very shy,
And he knew if he went in front of
the sheep, he'd blush sky high.
So off he went behind old Tara hill
the beauty,
And there he sighed, and duly did
his duty.

And coming back with a bladder free
of care,
Japers, in disbelief, our believer he
did stare.
For by all that was holy in that place
called Babalon
One of Paddy's little flock, Louie the
Lamb, was gone

For the wolf was also watching,
closely night and day

And as soon as Paddy off to Tara
walked away,
He leapt out with speed that was so
bleeding amazing,
And lifted poor Louie lamb in the
middle of his grazing.

Poor Paddy raised his holy hands on
high,
And to the Lord above did cry,
"Please Lord don't do this to me!
"I only went to taker a wee."

And then the sky in thunder broke,
and to St Paddy an Angel spoke,
"Don't worry Paddy. Don't for a
minute care.
"The Lord himself has heard your
prayer."

And as true as Murphy's stout is
good,
Out came the wolf from out the
wood
And acting like a repentant vandal,
Dropped Louie lamb at Paddy's
sandal

And said, "I'm sorry Paddy,"as
Louie to him did shove,
"I didn't know you were friends with
Him above."
And nodded his head as away did
run.
Today instead, he'd dine on venison.

And now on St. Patricks Day, with
crubeens and pints of beer,
We wish each other "Sláinte" and St
Patricks cheer.
And that's why all Irish scholars,
unless they are a glutton,
Eat corn beef and cabbage, and not
St Paddy's holy mutton.

THE PARTING GLASS *(traditional)*

"The Parting Glass" has been known as an Irish song of farewell for the past three centuries. The "parting glass" is the last drink a group shares together before they must part.

[Chorus]

  Dm   F   C

So fill to me the parting glass.

       Dm   Am   Dm

Good night, and joy be with you all.

[Third Verse Chorus]

I'll gently rise and I'll softly call,

"Goodnight and joy be with you all!"

   Dm   F   C   Dm   C

Of all the money that ever I had, I spent it in good company.

   Dm   F   C   Dm Am   Dm

And all the harm that ever I've done, alas, it was to none but me.

     F   Bb   Dm   Am

And all I've done for want of wit, to memory now, I can't recall.

[2]

If I had money enough to spend, and leisure time to sit awhile,

There is a fair maid in this town, that sorely has my heart beguiled.

Her rosy cheeks and ruby lips, I own, she has my heart in thrall.

[3]

Oh, all the comrades that ere I had, are sorry for my going away.

And all the sweethearts that ere I had, would wish me one more day to stay.

But since it falls unto my lot, that I should rise and you should not,

[4]

So fill to me, the parting glass, and drink a health, what ere befall,

I'll gently rise and I'll softly call, "Goodnight and joy be with you all!"

About the Rogues & Wenches

A mere decade ago Robert and Lucia Woofter met fellow actor, Benjamin James, during a rehearsal for the pirate pub show performed in the "Crooked Toad Tavern," which is staged at Anchorage's annual Three Barons Renaissance Fair. These three had such a high time performing in the tavern they decided to extend the fun and perform year 'round and not just in the first two weekends in June.

This motley crew soon discovered that they shared two strong predilections: an appreciation of fine ale and a love of the Irish song tradition. Those two components became the hallmarks of the fledgling band. For this reason you'll not see Rogues & Wenches performing without their silver mugs near to hand.

Hunter Woofter, already a seasoned performer for the preceding ten summers, joined the band at the age of fourteen as the percussionist after having mastered the Irish hand-held drum, the bodhran. Rogues & Wenches' Irish Linnet, Erin Kathleen Wells, joined the merry band the following summer, performing for her first time with Rogues & Wenches at the Scottish Highland Games. The band gave Erin a generous sixteen hours to learn the forty-odd songs Rogues & Wenches were performing at the games.

Our newest band member, Rebecca Gamache, was recruited for the band during a wedding at which Rogues & Wenches performed. While awaiting the arrival of the bride at the groom's family home a siren's voice could be heard from the kitchen drifting on the air, which was perfumed with the fragrance of fresh baked bread. Little did Rebecca know that her audition was complete and we wanted "that voice" for our troupe. Schooled in musical theater with a love of the classics, Rebecca agreed to join our merry band. She plays tin whistle and embellishes our performances with her lilting soprano voice.

Rogues & Wenches recorded their freshman and sophomore albums in Kevin Barnett's "Lovin' Dog Studio." The band is back in the studio with Kevin Barnett at Mirror Studios, working on their third CD, "Three Sheets to the Wind", a rowdy, rousing collection sea shanties & drinking songs.

In celebration of ten years of creative companionship and extensive performance in Anchorage and other Alaskan communities, Rogues & Wenches decided to make a pilgrimage to the source of their musical inspiration, Ireland, and have invited forty of their closest new fans and old friends to come along for the party! Thus the Rogues & Wenches Ireland Tour 2013 was born... and reborn in 2015!

About Philip M. Price

Philip M. Price is a professor at the University of Alaska Anchorage by day and a dulcet-toned balladeer by night. A native of Dublin, Ireland, Philip has been singing to and delighting audiences across Ireland, England, the rest of Europe, the United States, South America, and Central Asia for the past forty seven years. He has been described by his fans as "brilliant," "the real deal" and "the Irish Elvis."

About the NonMusical Authors

DARRELL LEWIS is a lifelong Alaskan, currently earning his MED in Teaching and Learning at the University of Alaska Anchorage. He is the Regional Historian for the National Register Program in National Park Service, Alaska Regional Office in Anchorage, Alaska. In this position he coordinates Alaska's National History Day program and provides historic preservation technical assistance to the state's National Historic Landmark owners.

N.J. HARRISON is an author, independent publisher, and the long-suffering wife of Philip M. Price. When not traveling, writing, or taking pictures of food, she can be found thinking about zombies and watching bad movies.

Alphabetical Index of Songs

Listed below are the songs and poem found in the pages of this book. After each song title is a key to which artist sings that song. All Rogues & Wenches songs are followed by "RW" and all Philip M. Price songs are followed by "PMP."

www.ingramcontent.com/pod-product-compliance
Lightning Source LLC
La Vergne TN
LVHW051810080426
835513LV00017B/1895

* 9 7 8 1 9 3 4 2 3 1 0 6 7 *